CHOSEN

TO

CHANNEL

Chosen To Channel
By MURIEL HOFF

Copyright 2017 by Muriel Hoff
All rights reserved, including the right of reproduction in whole or in part in any form.

Edited by Muriel Hoff & David Hoff

Foreword by Yossi Klein Halevi

Published by
David Hoff
Burning Bush Card Company
674 Prospect Avenue Suite 302 Hartford, Connecticut 06105
dhoff@sbcglobal.net

For information on written reprints,
book orders, readings, signings, and lectures please contact
David Hoff

First Edition 2017

Books By Muriel Hoff

Messages Via Muriel
The Voice in The Middle of The Night
Inspired Poems From The Universe
Animal Alphabet Rhymes For Children Up To 90

Poetry Also Appearing
In The Following Anthologies:

More Than Magnolias
Writer's Choice
Women Of The Piedmont Triad
Edge Of Our World
A Turn In Time
The Voice Within
Wordworks
Fire And Chocolate
Soundings Of Poetry
North Carolina's 400 Years
Signs Along The Way
Here's To The Land

Acknowledgements

My eternal thanks and gratitude to my late husband George for his love, support and patience from the beginning of my spiritual journey into the creative process that resulted in this book as well as my other books "Messages Via Muriel", "The Voice in The Middle of The Night", and "Inspired Poems from the Universe".

With love to my children, Cindy, Steve, David, and in memory of my daughter Rio. Thanks to my daughter-in-law Nina, my wonderful granddaughter Esther, and my son-in-law Dan and his wife Mariana.

My special thanks to my son David for his support and faith in my poetry and all the hours spent on compiling and editing this book.

Thank you to Jamie Furches for her proofreading of my manuscript.

Thank you to Yossi Klein Halevi for his support of my poetry and honoring me in writing the foreword.

Muriel Hoff

In memory of
Matthew Eisenfeld and Sara Duker.
Matt loved poetry and hoped
he and Sara
would have the opportunity to live
their lives as a poem.

Unfortunately while in Jerusalem
as a rabbinical student,
Matt and his girlfriend Sara
were killed in a 1996 terrorist attack.

Their lives continue
to be a blessing
for us, their survivors.

Muriel Hoff – An Appreciation

by Yossi Klein Halevi

Several years ago, David Hoff, a man I met when I did a speaking engagement at Beth El Temple in West Hartford, Connecticut gave me a batch of poems, explaining that they were written by his mother, Muriel. And, he added, if you are interested I will be happy to send you more. After reading these poems I was more than interested – I was intrigued and deeply moved.

And so began a long-distance relationship in which, from time to time, I would receive a new batch of Muriel's poems from David. And each time I was inspired anew.

All poets are lovers, hopeless romantics, and Muriel Hoff is a great lover. Her love is the Jewish people—it's history, traditions and reborn homeland. These are poems that barely contain the quivering heart that wrote them; one often feels that her words are over-whelmed by their own emotional urgency.

The Jewish tradition that resonates most deeply for Muriel is the voice of the prophets, their vision of redemption. Muriel longs for the prophet who was "Bold and arrogant, yet humble as the dust," a voice for "the words of the Lord, mouthing them with discomfort and anxiety, the coals burning."

Muriel understands the conflicted soul of the prophet, who feels discomfort and anxiety precisely because he loves his people, yet must rebuke them. Not only is the prophet's mission rooted in paradox, but so too is his message: "Mirror of hope, and well of happiness, conveyor of sorrow and misery."

Muriel's poems recall the prayerful essence of classical Jewish poetry. "Say a psalm," urges the poet. "Say it in the morning. Say it in the night. Say it soft with pleasure. Savor its delight."

These poems are themselves small psalms, reminders that in the absence of prophets, we rely on our poets to awaken in us a longing for God.

Reading Muriel Hoff evokes for me that great primitivist painter, Shalom of Safed, whose naïve and loving renditions of biblical stories restored them to freshness. Like Shalom, Muriel's innocence conceals a keen awareness of the pathologies of this world, along with a refusal to accept the world as it is.

The poet writes: "Messiah will come when there is a readiness of heart, a willingness to abandon heresy, a feeling of brother-sister love." Muriel implies a stunning new definition of heresy: the absence of heart, of brother-sister love. The response to that heresy, and the key to redemption, is love.

Muriel Hoff's poetic mission is to remind us of our purpose: to bring God's light and expansive vision to a broken world, and to refuse to accept the world on its own terms.

Yossi Klein Halevi
Senior Fellow at the Shalom Hartman Institute in Jerusalem

Long-time journalist and author of three books, including LIKE DREAMERS, which won the Jewish Book Council's 2013 Everett Award for Jewish book of the year

INTRODUCTION

    I am really excited about my newest book of inspired poems entitled "Chosen To Channel". It is my fourth book from my channeling experiences. The other books are "<u>Messages Via Muriel</u>", "<u>The Voice in the Middle of the Night</u>", and "<u>Inspired Poems from the Universe</u>". All my poetry was channeled from the most inspirational and challenging inner revelations of my lifetime.

    I began to experience myself opening up to new levels of heightened sensitivity and perception while taking a course on the Psychology of Creativity. I began noticing peculiar sensations such as the skin of my face flushing although my temperature was normal, squinting to read as if I had become light sensitive, and overwhelming feelings of universal love that often brought tears. I later learned that these were physical signs that were the beginning of a creative process.

    I believe that channeling is an accurate term for the activity of my creative process. When this channeling process began, I would find myself awakened during the late night hours by a voice in my head reciting one or two lines of poetry. I strongly felt as if I was commanded to get out of bed and see if other lines of poetry would follow. I would take a pen and a sheet of paper or the cardboard from a new pantyhose package and then go into a dimly lit room keeping my eyes half closed so I wouldn't be completely awakened and ready to go back to sleep.

In my first experience of this nighttime channeling, I began writing the first line I had heard when a strange thing occurred. I felt the pen start to move by itself and the words tumbled out as if I was taking dictation from an invisible source. As I finished one poem, then another poem would start on a different subject and others would follow until the entire sheet of paper was full. I would even write in all the margins.

The next day I typed up what I had written and though some words were scribbled, I could figure them out. The titles of the poems were always added afterwards.

I honestly feel that these inspired poems were given to me as a gift, and I also know that the reason I was chosen to receive them was to enable me to give this gift back to you, and you, and you. Enjoy.

Muriel Hoff
Greensboro, North Carolina

CONTENTS

Protecting The Holy Land	1
Secret of Jewish Spiritual Survival	2,3
A Melody of Words	4
Search Well	5
Halacha	6
The Challenge	7
When Messiah Comes	8
Haifa	9
The Eternal Jew	10,11
Entering The Bible	12
Chanukah Lights	13
Hineni	14
Renewal Of Israel	15
Tradition	16,17
Open Your Heart To Me	18
The Rabbi	19
Where Does It All Fit Together	20
Do Not Forsake Us	21
Tefillin	22
Israel Beckons	23
Say A Psalm	24
The Sound Of The Shofar	25

A Little Bit Of Messiah	26
Doing The Mitzvah	27
Shavuot	28
Torah	29
We Are One	30
Splendor Of Shabbat	31
Eternal Message	32
Indestructible Document	33
Words Of Rashi	34
Kaddish	35
Christians Working With Jews	36
Healing Waters Of The Mikveh	37
Esther	38
Shabbat-A Jewel In The Crown	39
Moses	40
Jerusalem	41
The Approach Of Shabbat	42
The Glory Of Torah	43,44
Light Up The World	45
Hope	46
Maimonides	47
Israel Is Mourning	48
The Lord's Precepts	49
Days Of Remembrance	50

Tzedakah	51
A Remnant Of Our People	52
The Scribe	53
Malachi, Oh Malachi	54
Lest They Forget	55
The Plea and The Answer	56,57
The Old Jew	58
Oh Israel	59
The Prophet	60
Say The Shema	61
Awash In Loveliness	62
Soul To Soul	63
When Messiah Comes	64,65,66
Israel Welcomes You	67
Come Unto Me	68
Remember and Reconsider	69
Hidden Secrets	70
A New Day	71
Healed Again and Again	72
To Be A Hostage	73
The Potential For Greatness	74
Messiah Is Coming	75
The Western Wall	76, 77
Goodness And Tenderness	78

PROTECTING THE HOLY LAND

We pause to observe the difficulties
of just existing on this earth.

Thrust upon us
is this great responsibility.
The burden is
heavy on our shoulders.
It presses us down,
but at the same time lifts us up,
for we are soldiers of the Lord
protecting the holy land that was
given to us when God willed
it to Abraham.

The covenant is clear.
The writing stands on the wall.
The task is great, but we shall not
slacken in our duty.
Arise oh ye Israel,
and hold your banner high.

SECRET OF JEWISH SPIRITUAL SURVIVAL

The Dalai Lama asked:
*"Tell me your secret, the secret of
Jewish spiritual survival in exile?"*

When we were slaves,
God led us in the right direction.
We were weak,
but He made us strong.
Our task was to listen
and many of us faltered.

He made a path for us
and set down the Law.
All we had to do was obey.

God's hand has stayed with us
throughout history leading us
in the right direction.

He told us to love, be merciful
and be compassionate.
Want not only material things
but offer service of the heart.

Be proud, but not overbearing.
Ride not the wild herd,
but travel the middle road.
Let anger be your foe,
and speak with equanimity,

quietly acknowledging
the good in people.

Wisdom is doled out and
to receive it one must be worthy.
To be uninhibited and willful is
destructive and not in your favor.

A MELODY OF WORDS

```
         The Torah
    own.         goes
    very         around
     its         and
all              around
  a melody       and
    sings        every
          word
```

SEARCH WELL

Rays of light glimmer
through the darkness.
Hope and faith imminently
go hand in hand.
In Israel lies the answer
to questions left unanswered.
In the tombs of the past lie
the keys to the future.
Search well for the time is short
and your destiny awaits.
Embrace your heritage,
impress it upon your mind
and the results will be
unfathomable and penetrating.
Hold tight to the present,
for the answer lies
wedged in between.
Accept graciously the immense
pleasure and sensory perceptions.
Put yourself to the test
and you will come out
with shining colors.

HALACHA

Halacha is for the observant Jew,

the cry to centuries of living

a rigorous traditional way of life.

It spells out the duties

and obligations expounded

by the Lord to Moses

when He gave His covenant

to the people Israel.

THE CHALLENGE

Israel is tied to the land
in such a way that it is almost
unacceptable to separate them.

The land is the nourishment from
which the Israelites gleaned the
courage to go forward.

The task of the redemption of Israel
has always been the chief desire of
the early settlers.

Take the challenge and hold it high,
for it glimmers and gleams.
Ah yes, it is holy.

WHEN MESSIAH COMES

Messiah will come when there is
a readiness of heart,
a willingness to abandon heresy,
a desire to be as one with God,
a knowing deep within that
all is right in the world,
a feeling of fellow-man love,
a feeling of brother-sister love,
a feeling of awe and amazement
at all the wonders God has placed
at our feet.

A complete abandonment of
desire for power over people,
over the earth, but surrender to
knowing the vital force that
connects us to the mightiest,
the all loving, all encompassing
Father, the King of Kings.
May our spirits unite and blend,
may Messiah feel a new worthiness
of receiving and giving,
and may our paths be peace.

HAIFA

Haifa

jewel of the sea,

mistress of the harbor

waiting for her lover,

in her nightgown of shining lights.

THE ETERNAL JEW

I am the voice of the Eternal Jew.
Deep within my being
I hear the words:
Take heed my people—have you
forgotten the wanderings,
the sufferings, the wars,
the pogroms, the Holocaust?
Life is so tranquil.
Doors of acceptance
open all around you.
A sea of complacency swells and
disintegrates our strength.
We are thus weakened
and become vulnerable.
At Mt. Sinai we were given
the Torah.
We must see that it is
passed on to future generations.
Living in your present,
you forget your past.
When you soften your guard
you weaken, and erosion
tears the fabric of your being.
The warning is clear.
Beware of drowning
in a sea of forgetfulness.
We are the keepers
of the Eternal Light.

We are the guardians of our past.
We are the stewards of our future.
Brand this word on your soul:
Remember   Remember   Remember

ENTERING THE BIBLE

I want to enter the Bible
slowly and with caution,
toe in first, then ankle
wading in slowly,
till I am knee deep,
and then the waist.
At this point
I know I will take the leap
and throw myself in completely,
to be enveloped in the swirling
turbulent water,
at the mercy of history.

CHANUKAH LIGHTS

Chanukah lights shine,
shine your glory on me,
forge molten memories
of Jewish history past,
Judah and his tiny
band of Maccabees.
Menorah lights blaze,
eight nights of remembrance.
Remember the tyrant Antiochus,
and how justice
triumphed over iniquity.
Candelabra glow,
kindle the candles bright.
Relive the miracle
of Chanukah
this 25th day of Kislev.
Fill the world with Light.

HINENI

Hineni.
Here I am,
ready to take action,
to take up the challenge,
to expedite the situation,
to make peace
where there has been war,
but where are You?

I cannot hear you.
I wait for your prayer.
I hear faint stirrings.

RENEWAL OF ISRAEL

Speaking of miracles
isn't the renewal of Israel
a great miracle?
Out of the wilderness
a people forged together
a great nation.
With God's aid they tore into
a task almost inhumanly possible
to fulfill.
They carved out of stone
a retreat for all Jews,
a safety zone where laughter and joy
rang out despite adversity.
Where men and women shouldered
the task of fighting a relentless
enemy, surrounded on all sides
by mortar and shells.

TRADITION

Civilizations fade and slip
away into eternity.

The Jews always emerge
to continue their tradition
and renew their covenant with God.

It is a pattern set and constantly
followed through the centuries.

The emergence of a holy person
in the guise of man
brands the word of God
into the hearts of Jews
for now and forevermore.

Morally, we are the
people of the Book.

We are duty bound
to help our neighbors,
and seek atonement
for he who does wrong.

Compassion and mercy is the tag
we wear in our hearts.

Love of God shines from within
and its rays emanate.

A holy person
has that special glow
about him and
is a joy to behold.
To be in his presence
is to be blessed.

OPEN YOUR HEART TO ME

I have chosen your people
as my people.
I have chosen to follow
in the path of Sarah, Rebekah,
Rachel and Leah.
Like a flower needs
sunlight and dew,
without your acceptance
and encouragement,
I wither, and feel
worthless and unfulfilled.
If you open your
heart to me,
I will work for
the advancement of our people
and our reward shall
be on earth
and in heaven.

THE RABBI

The Rabbi must be humble.
His position was given to him as an honor and he must bend his knee to the King. Although he is a priest of the most Holy on high, he must remain as an ash that can blow away at the whim and caprice of the forces of nature governed by the most Holy of Holies. There are those who believe that a Rabbi is above all. He is there to please God by doing the commandments in the Torah- mainly to love justice, mercy, and walk humbly in the path of his maker.

WHERE DOES IT All FIT TOGETHER

What does it mean to be a Jew?
To wander for centuries,
to pick scrupulously at the laws
searching for a hidden
morsel of wisdom.
Where does it all fit together?
What is the stream
that continuously ebbs
and then refreshes itself?

DO NOT FORSAKE US

Israel oh Israel.
Do not forsake us dear Lord, a
nation scattered but not shattered.
We will assess our fortune to fight,
for in our forbearance is strength.
Moral character we have,
stamina we have.
We need the Lord.
Without the Lord we are lost.
If He leads our legion,
behind Him we stand united.
God is our shield,
our armor, our love.
We are humble servants,
for He has chosen us to be
His people and we
stand ready to serve Him
as the martyrs served Him.
We are prepared to go,
but spare us dear Lord.
Bring us victory.
Let not a mother's tears be shed,
for the villainy is not deserving
that she should cry.

TEFILLIN

Tefillin carries with it a tradition
long past but never ending.
The mysteries of the universe unfold
in awesome progression.

Cherish your values.
Hold fast the tradition.
The rewards are boundless.
They lay in waiting
to be revived by your touch.

The ancient tradition of tefillin
merges the mysteries of the past
with the present and future.

Anon and anon and anon.

Tefillin holds fast the traditions of
days long past, bringing to the
devoted and dedicated a way of life
that goes back thousands of years.
Centuries fall away, and you stand a
loyal subject of Israel, beholden only
to God, and feeling His presence fills
you with worth and wellbeing.

ISRAEL BECKONS

Israel beckons.
I must answer.
I feel it
in my gut.
My destiny
awaits me there.

SAY A PSALM

Say a psalm.
Say it in the morning.
Say it in the night.
Say it soft with pleasure.
Savor its delight.

Let it overcome you.
Let your spirit rise.
Let it work its magic.
Lift you to the skies.

THE SOUND OF THE SHOFAR

Tekiah, shevarim-teruah, tekiah
Tekiah, shevarim, tekiah
Tekiah, teruah
Tekiah gedolah

It echoes deep within the Jewish
soul, a summons to action,
awakening us as from a
deep slumber, alerting us
that the time is now.

Tekiah, shevarim-teruah, tekiah
Tekiah, shevarim, tekiah
Tekiah, teruah
Tekiah gedolah

This ancient cry has
survived to modernity.
Listen to its warning.
Take notice and take heed.
This people we hold so dear must be
guarded as a great treasure,
greater than gold, greater
than precious jewels.
This people Israel must survive.

A LITTLE BIT OF MESSIAH

There is a little bit of Messiah
in each of us.
 A treasure waiting to be found.
Dig down deep, search your soul
patiently with humility.
Eventually you will find that
little bit of Messiah
that God has planted
in everyone of us,
and when you find it,
rise to the occasion and
leave your fingerprints
on the map of humanity.

DOING THE MITZVAH

Although we think and meditate,
it is action that counts.
While words are beautiful,
sometimes they are empty,
but the person who acts
brings realization to the word.
While doing the mitzvah,
the good deed, a rainbow
often bursts in our midst.
It makes us suddenly aware
of our own ineptitudes,
and lack of a firm commitment.
It gives us the liftoff to action,
for truly the gift is received after
the action has been transacted,
and in giving you receive,
and receive, and receive.

SHAVUOT

           mountain
        holy   and
         His   we
      unto   will
        up   sing
     go   and
     us   dance
   let   and
Come   write
love songs to the Lord.

Count not the

infinitesimal beginnings.

Compare them only to the

grandeur of the movable feast.

TORAH

Torah,
the book of God.

Torah,
the heavenly word.

Torah,
the shield of a nation.

Torah,
the light of a
million tomorrows.

Torah,
the destiny of a people.

Torah,
the wisdom of the ages.

Torah,
binding up the wounds
and healing them.

Torah,
raising up children to follow
in the footsteps of parents.
Torah,
a blessing from the Lord.

WE ARE ONE

This land, holy of holies,
haven for the homeless,
this State of Israel, small in size,
but a giant in spirit,
has captured our hearts,
and fired our imaginations.
As she takes us into her bosom
we feel her agonies, her anguish,
and the pride of
her many accomplishments.
We have trod her soil,
studied her history,
realized her ambitions, her fears,
and walked in the footsteps
of her heroes.
We take back to America
memories of a shared experience
of laughter and tears,
and the knowledge born anew,
that we are one.
Though we cannot complete the task
we must persevere,
and with God's help
make the dream a reality.

SPLENDOR OF SHABBAT

All my tensions are erased
and flow away
as I surrender myself
to your beauty,
our Sabbath Queen.

I step into the past
and become a part of the eternity
of my people,
and emerge cleansed
and ready to face
the challenge of modernity.

There never was and there
will never be anything as beautiful
as the splendor of Shabbat.

ETERNAL MESSAGE

Burning, burning, burning,

the word of God

inflames my soul,

searing like a live coal

imprinting the eternal message.

INDESTRUCTIBLE DOCUMENT

The commandments come
    Knocking,
        Knocking,
            Pounding,
                Resounding
        "Thou shall, thou shall not."

Indestructible document hewn
  by the hand of the Lord,
    given by Moses the messenger.

The slumbering soul awakens,
pushes away the cobwebs,
and as dust disintegrates
the neshama
      Remembers,
         Remembers,
            Remembers.

WORDS OF RASHI

Rashi says,
and the world listens
to the words
lean and lucid,
terse verse,
cementing centuries,
linking a people
to its past.

KADDISH

Lest we forget
the six million
Jews who perished
during the Holocaust,
I will say Kaddish.

One person speaking out,
a formal renunciation of the heinous
crimes committed.
The madness of a German
generation hypnotized, in awe of a
mass murderer and following like
puppets on a string.

I am every man, every woman,
angered, anguished, expecting
nothing, only the opportunity to
humbly say this prayer.
My heart beats six million,
six million, six million.
I care, I hurt, I grieve,
and feeling these pangs,
I say Kaddish.

CHRISTIANS WORKING WITH JEWS

Christians working with Jews
can make it happen.
A better world, a peaceful world,
a world of love and affection,
of brotherhood,
of linking of arms,
shoulder to shoulder,
pushing together to crumble
hate, ignorance,
infamy and ingratitude,
easing the pain
and making the task
immeasurably softer.
The time will come when
brothers will face each other
across the dining table
and praise the Lord
loud and clear in unison.
The world will be a lovely place,
the earth will be sweet,
and joy will reign
throughout the land.

HEALING WATERS OF THE MIKVEH

To immerse oneself in the
rippling waters of the mikveh
is to feel the sacredness
of the moment and the peacefulness
of sanctification.

Renewal is achieved by
submission to the purity
of the healing waters,
and the joyful awakenings
that ennoble the spirit and
change you forever.

ESTHER

ESTHER,
handmaiden of the Lord,
daughter of Israel
a joy to her people.

ESTHER,
crowned with beauty,
majestic as myrtle,
destined to be Queen.

ESTHER,
bedazzled King Achashverosh,
befuddled traitor Haman,
raised up by wise Mordecai.

AT PURIM
read the megillah scroll,
rattle noisemakers loudly,
rejoice with gift giving,
revel in gay costumery,
remember the heroine who
rescued the Jews of Shushan.
ESTHER

SHABBAT- A JEWEL IN THE CROWN

The Shabbat is a jewel
in the crown of the Lord.
Participating in the
Sabbath service and
singing His praises,
you become a facet
in the gleaming
of His light,
reflecting His glory.

MOSES

Moses was the bearer
of many messages.
Into his hands fell the knowledge
that was to turn the tide
in the affairs of men.
Concurrent with events and running
through the sands of time,
his dialogue with the Lord remains
the most prevalent in history.
Timeless and all expanding,
bringing us closer to one another,
giving us hope in a time of madness
and uncertainty.
Moses drew people to him like a
magnet. His words came to the
uninitiated and settled like a cloud
on a misty day that lifts and
dispels the gloom.

JERUSALEM

I know Jerusalem,
and yet I know her not.
She is as elusive to me as a slave
girl running away from her master.
For three nights she throbbed
in my blood, and
swam through my head,
and yet she is aloof
holding herself at a distance.
I will be a patient suitor
but when she surrenders to me,
I pray I capture her true beauty,
for she is indeed a prize,
a precious jewel.

THE APPROACH OF SHABBAT

I feel Shabbat approaching.
Not by the date on the calendar,
but by the quickening of my heart.
There comes over me a longing
to be one with my God,
to pick up the Book,
to explore the mystery
of how and why
I feel special being a Jew.

THE GLORY OF THE TORAH

To be called up to the Torah
is indeed an honor.
Within the Torah lie many secrets
handed down from
generation to generation.
The Torah swells with buoyancy
and resounds with
the rhythms of centuries
of living.
Within its portals
are the mysteries
that burn their way
into our hearts and
leave an indelible bond.
To be close to the Torah
is to feel the glory
and know true peace.
A finger of Torah
is worth more
than the greatest slice of life,
for it is life itself.
Within its contents lay all heart
rendering details to uplift the soul
and make it true.

Divine Light emanates therefrom
and to hover near brings you closer
and closer to God.

His powers are magnificent.
He causes the earth to tremble,
the winds to whistle,
and the seas to roar.
Indeed He is mighty.
Oh compassionate One,
take me to You.
I entrust my heart,
knowing it is in Your hands,
and that You will
allow me to be a free
and independent person.
For God wants to see His children
emeshed in the problems of society,
searching for answers.
If you call upon Him for help,
He will be there.
He waits.
Don't ignore Him.
God is very sensitive,
and His feelings are easily hurt.
He waits for you
with open arms
and forgives,
and forgives true seekers,
even though they
may occasionally stray.

LIGHT UP THE WORLD

God casts a mighty shadow
all over the world.

Man steps in the shadow
and is blessed.

Blessed with a responsibility
to carry on deeds of valor,
to lighten the load of the oppressed,
to light up the world,
to make His glory known,
to cause tremendous changes,
to feel at ease,
be a good person and a good Jew.

HOPE

Hope is that little voice
that won't be put down,
that sends shivers up the spine,
in anticipation of something big
about to happen.

Hope is the staff of courage
that you lean upon
when you're feeling down and out.

You don't need a barrel of hope,
just one tiny spark,
to keep the fire burning.

Like the Eternal Light
it should never go out.

MAIMONIDES

Oh Maimonides, Maimonides,
the circumference of the earth
cannot encompass the
girth of your knowledge.
You absorbed history, and
once inside the brilliant metal
of your mind, it was melted
down and fragmented.
Separating wheat from chaff,
you tied it into beautiful sheaves.
Euclidic in nature,
indifferent to affectation
no problem was too abstract.
Your mind was a nimble gazelle
dancing on slippery rocks.
With eternal patience you
pieced together puzzles of
catastrophic dimensions.
Connecting past with present
the hidden emerged
under your microscope.
The light of a thousand stars
shined from within.
Indeed you were a holy man.

ISRAEL IS IN MOURNING

Israel is in mourning.
Will you not come
to lay roses at the graves
of those who died
in honor and glory?
Will you not cry at the Wall?
Will you not pay homage with the
rest of the searching souls?

THE LORD'S PRECEPTS

Blessed are they who follow the
precepts of the Lord.
Blessed are the children who walk
in the ways of the Lord.
They fulfill His mission,
and in so doing carry on a tradition
that lasts forever.
They were told at Mount Sinai
that theirs was a peculiar,
but particular mission.
This was the way to show the world
the leadership of a King,
who governed without a country,
but who knows all,
and rewards those
who follow His laws.
As mysterious as He is,
His motives are clear.
Complete faith and adherence
to His law is demanded.
Yet if you falter,
you are still loved,
and if you plead for forgiveness
you will be forgiven.
His will is divine.
Advance in the knowledge that
He is the one
and only God.
Hallowed be His name.

DAYS OF REMEMBRANCE

On these days of days,
days of remembrance,
repentance, and return,
let us not forget our Creator.
With a full heart, let us ask
forgiveness for our sins
and pay penance in
humble humility,
praying for God's love and light
to close the bond between us.
How far, but how near,
a breath away.

TZEDAKAH

Tzedakah is indeed
a gift of the heart.
A blessing
of benevolent behavior,
and an act of conscience.
Therefore, again and again,
open your heart to the stranger.
Show love, pity and compassion.

A REMNANT OF OUR PEOPLE

And it shall come to pass
that there will come
amongst us a remnant of our people
from long ago and far away.

They shall be many colors
and speak many tongues.

They shall know without
knowing why, and they shall do
what their hearts tell them is right.

God will look and say:
Ah, My people have returned at last.

THE SCRIBE

The sofer writes
and in respect
to what he writes
he is a constituent
of a time past yet present,
and growing in stature.

He continues
a tradition of respect
to the word,
and a combination
of faith and destiny.

A hewer in the stone,
a combatant against the destruction
of a tradition.

Rich and glowing,
a rememberer of the glory
of a people embroiled in a struggle,
who made their mark in history.

MALACHI OH MALACHI

Malachi, Malachi,
messenger of My mouth,
silver-tongued appointee,
heralding the apparition
of things to come,
harbinger of omens,
witness to the facts.
Go forth and take the message
to the people.
Tarry not, fire men into action
to stand up and be counted.
Prophesy, oh Malachi
Prophesy, My word.

LEST THEY FORGET

Remember the six million…
the Holocaust,
victims of a madman's evil dream.
This tree must not bear fruit.
This volcano must not erupt again.
Tell it to your children
and they to their children.
Imprint it in their minds,
implant it in their souls,
generation to generation
lest they forget,
lest they forget.

THE PLEA AND THE ANSWER

Do not forsake us dear Lord,
as we stand dejected and lonely,
we are never cowards.

In our hearts burn the
flame of liberty and justice.

Was it not decreed at Mt. Sinai
that we were bound to You
by an eternal covenant?

Feeling thus loved by the King of all,
how could we abandon our faith?

Yet in desperate situations,
again and again,
the world turns against us,
their purpose to wipe us out.

Is annihilation of the Jews
from the face of the earth
our tragic inheritance?
Won't there come a time
when there will be peace?

THE ANSWER

My people, My people,
let the yoke fall!
Surrounded as you are
by enemies and alien thoughts,
I am with you.
My mighty arm will protect you.
How can I desert what is My own?
Though I am hidden
and can't be seen,
My sparks are within each of you.
For was it not Abraham,
who bound his son
and offered him to Me?
Did he not show his love?
I am your Father, your Brother,
and your Friend, but our love
withers if you do not call Me.
Like a suckling without milk,
like a tender shoot without rain.
Come to Me,
and I will open new avenues.
Together we will fight and
win the victory.

THE OLD JEW

The old Jew
sits in the waning light,
magnifying glass in hand.
A humped question mark
poring over the pages
of his beloved Talmud.
His wispy white beard
feathering the weathered words,
rocking forward, rocking backward,
chanting, memorizing,
squirreling away his treasure
for the long dark days ahead.

OH ISRAEL

Oh Israel,
how you have attached yourself
to my heartstrings.

I breathe your air
and my lungs are filled
to bursting.

My heart pounds
with a strange new love
of devotion and fraternity.

THE PROPHET

What manner of man
was the prophet?

Bold and arrogant, yet
humble as the dust.
A token of justice, mercy,
compassion, and faith,
reciting over and over again
the words of the Lord,
mouthing them with discomfort
and anxiety, the coals burning.

Mirror of hope, and well of
happiness, conveyor of
sorrow and misery.

Maximum security could not
deter him. He had to speak
for he was so empowered
to carry forth to the nations
the monument to a new tomorrow.

Misery was his garden
and he planted seeds
to ferment the population to action.

Alabaster and steel,
with a heart of gold,
go forth and proclaim
the message of the Lord.

Awake the populace.

SAY THE SHEMA

Say the Shema.
Say it in the morning.
Say it in the evening.
Say it whenever you feel
the need arises.
These are the words:
Shema Yisrael,
Adonai Eloheinu
Adonai echad.
Men have clung to these words,
and martyrs have left the world
with these words on their lips.

It is a code of honor
between yourself and the Lord,
binding you together in a knot
of passionate love and faith.

AWASH IN LOVELINESS

I feel blessed, awash in the
loveliness of Shabbat.
I feel a glowing radiance enmeshed
in the specialness of this night,
the magic of the moment.
How to explain but to say,
"Ah yes, ah yes, the Lord reaches
out and you can feel His presence,
and it is lovely."

To be a Jew is indeed an honor.
A member of a special tribe
whose destiny is determined
and mapped out by a power
higher than the stars,
mightier than the mountains,
and yet as small as the tiniest seed
that grows and grows
into a lovely flower.
In renewal is found
the secret ingredient.
In returning you feel
you have come home at last.

SOUL TO SOUL

The Torah stretches
out its hand to you.
Come to me,
become a part of me,
rub yourself against the
fabric of my cloth.
Invade my heart.
Meet me soul to soul.
Step into my portals.
You will never be the same.

WHEN MESSIAH COMES

When Messiah comes there will be
dancing in the streets,
and people will shine
with a radiance that
comes from within,
for they are imbued
with the spirit of the Lord.

It will be a joyous time
for neighbors shall give their energy,
time, and devotion to doing good
deeds to help each other,
and nary a sharp word
shall be heard between them.

They shall have patience and
understanding unseen before.

The Torah is imprinted
on their hearts.
Try as they may to not follow
its precepts, they are stopped
and turned in a new direction.
All people shall live in peace and
war shall be no more.

Tenderness, mercy, and regards of
the feelings of others shall be an
everyday experience.

It shall be good.
Yes, it shall be good.

It will be a time of spiritual
awakening and people will know
what they did not know before.
All the souls will mingle and
exchange ideas and knowledge.
There will be a renaissance
of learning.
Scholars will emerge
to lead the new generation.

There will be no need for courts
because everything can be settled
by going within and
hearing the small still voice.

People will work
and the air shall be pure,
the food pure,
and their sinews shall be
strong and endurable.

Love shall be in the air
and they shall inhale it.

It shall be said that this
is a time of great achievement.

Old souls will join the young
and carry out wondrous acts.

The world shall be joyous
for it is filled
with the spirit of the Lord.

Sparks shall light a fire in everyone
and they shall shine from within
because they are holy.

Happiness and joy
shall reign supreme
and the people will see
miracles with their own eyes
as they have never seen before.

The name of this time
shall be Messiah.

ISRAEL WELCOMES YOU

Freedom waits,
Israel welcomes you.
The sweetness
of the land will fulfill you.
You will be absorbed
into the melting pot,
and yet retain
your identity.
Let the earth
shake and tremble
from the many footsteps.
There is always room
for the children
of the Lord.

COME UNTO ME

Out of the wilderness
came the words:
Come unto me and
I will lay you down
a carpet of tender green shoots.
Thorns and thistles
will disappear and the
desert will emerge as a
Queen radiant and lovely.

REMEMBER AND RECONSIDER

REMEMBER:
You are a thread
in the holy fabric
of Jewish history.

RECONSIDER:
Change yourself
and you can
change the world.

HIDDEN SECRETS

Encyclopedias of knowledge
often fall short of
true meaning.

For deep
in the earth
are hidden many secrets.

Warriors of days past
have left no visible clues of the
mysteries surrounding the universe.

Eternally, it is man
acting in partnership with God,
who unravels these mysteries.

A NEW DAY

And so it shall come to pass:

The young and the innocent shall
go forth free, and no nation shall
be in shackles and appurtenant
to another.

Men shall lift their heads on a new day, a
day of glory where the fields and all things
that dwell within, the oxen as well as the
swine shall be as brothers, and the milk of
the land shall be as sweet as honey, and the
chaff shall remain ignored, for only good
thoughts of peace and harmony shall enter
the house of the Lord.

HEALED AGAIN AND AGAIN

A Jew is a Jew is a Jew
and beloved of God is he.
His mind must connect
on a higher level.
His feelings while visceral
must exude satisfaction
with his plight,
while not accepting
of the baser elements
of his soul that try
to dominate and rule him.
Let peace wander this earth
and man, a mimic of
yesterday's past, incur damages
to be healed again and again
by His light and His love.

TO BE A HOSTAGE

To have to pay for your life,
to be a hostage,
to have a price on your head,
to be a prisoner,
to know fear every minute,
to ache with the desire to be free,
to live under constant surveillance,
to undergo untold agonies
of the mind and spirit.
To look to Israel
with hopeful determination
knowing freedom waits in Israel
where the yoke will be lifted.

THE POTENTIAL FOR GREATNESS

God resides within
each and everyone of us.
He waits to reveal Himself in all His
glory, but first we have to reveal to
Him a mirror image of compassion,
mercy, and justice.
We all have the potential for
greatness, but the task demands
concentration, planning and hard
work.
We must be open to the natural
wonders God has given us,
and as His chosen people
we must support and nurture
the State of Israel.
If we are true to ourselves
in all these endeavors,
we may experience the awe,
and wonder of the God within.

MESSIAH IS COMING

Messiah is coming.
Ah yes, Messiah is coming.
Whisper it in the treetops,
shout it to the moon,
soon, soon Messiah is coming.

Can't you tell, listen well.
The air is filled with singing.
There's dancing in the streets.
Just you wait and see.
Soon, soon Messiah is coming.

Set for him a table
and invite the world to share.
Brothers, sisters come together,
never fear, listen here,
soon, soon Messiah is coming.

THE WESTERN WALL

It is said the divine spirit
rests upon the Western Wall,
Jerusalem, Israel,
holy remnant of destruction
of the second Temple, 70 C.E.
From distant shores they come,
the wealthy, the beggars,
the knowers, the seekers,
magnetized by the attraction
of this monument to history.
They come to study, pray,
meditate, making Shabbat
a special memory.
They insert notes in narrow
crevices of tear stained stones.
Prayers for the afflicted,
prayers for miracles,
prayers for peace.
Survivor of enemy imprisonment,
cursed, covered with garbage
and dung, stoically refusing
to surrender.
During the Six Day War,
Israeli parachutists
fell from the sky,
angels answering prayers,
rescuing and restoring
the rough hewn stones.

An ear, a heart,
a haven to all who seek solace,
the Western Wall offers compassion,
solemnity, hope, and joy.
May it reign in peace forever.

GOODNESS AND TENDERNESS

Goodness is from within the heart.
It flows like milk and honey
from the promised land.
Its rays are like the sun.
They shine and the
countenance reflects their rays.
Goodness is in reality
the freedom to express
from within the heart,
the innermost feelings
of tenderness.
Tenderness has magic powers
to melt frozen hearts and
bring joy to the world.
Tenderness holds dear
the innermost feelings
between man and woman
and binds them together
to form a union.
It encourages children to attain
great heights of ambition.
It is an aura that is warm,
shines like a halo
and oozes out
to soothe and heal.

INDEX

Abraham	1, 57
Bible	12
Chanukah	13
Christians	36
Covenant	1, 16
Dalai Lama	2
Days of Remembrance	50
Esther	38
Eternal Jew	10
Eternal Light	11, 46
Eternal Message	32
Haifa	9
Halacha	6
Hineni	14
Holocaust	10, 35, 55
Holy of Holies	19
Israel	1, 5, 6, 7, 15, 21, 22, 23, 30, 38, 48, 59, 66, 73, 74
Jerusalem	41, 76
Jewish History	69

Jewish Soul	25
Jewish Survival	2
Jews	6, 15, 16, 20, 35, 36, 42, 45, 56, 58, 62, 73
Jews of Shushan	38
Kaddish	35
King	19, 49
King of Kings	8
Leah	18
Maccabees	13
Maimonides	47
Malachi	54
Martyrs	21
Megillah Scroll	38
Menorah	13
Messiah	8, 26, 64, 75
Mikveh	37
Milk and Honey	78
Miracles	15
Mitzvah	27
Mordecai	38

Moses	6, 33, 40
Mount Sinai	10, 49, 56
Mysteries	70
Neshama	33
Prophet	60
Psalm	24
Purim	38
Rabbi	19
Rachel	18
Rashi	34
Rebekah	18
Sabbath Queen	31
Sarah	18
Shabbat	42, 62, 76
Shabbat Jewel	39
Shavuot	28
Shema	61
Six Day War	76
Small Still Voice	65
Sofer	53
Spirit of the Lord	64

Tefillin	22
Tekiah	25
Tzedakah	51
Torah	4, 10, 29, 43, 63, 64
Western Wall	48, 76

ABOUT THE AUTHOR

Muriel Hoff is a long time Greensboro, NC resident and is a member of the Writer's Group of the Triad.

Her first book of inspirational poetry, *Messages Via Muriel*, was published in 2003, *The Voice in the Middle of the Night* in 2006, and *Inspired Poems From the Universe* in 2013. Muriel and artist Emily Huntley published *Animal Alphabet Rhymes for Children up to Ninety* in 1985.

Her poetry has also appeared in the following anthologies:

The Greensboro Group: *More Than Magnolias, Writer's Choice, Women of the Piedmont Triad, Edge of Our World,* and *A Turn in Time*.

The Writer's Group of the Triad: *The Voice Within* and short stories in *Introspectrum: An Anthology of Personal Reflections, Wordworks, and Fire and Chocolate.*

The North Carolina Poetry Society: *Soundings of Poetry, North Carolina's 400 Years: Signs Along the Way,* and *Here's to the Land.*

Anthology of Magazine Verse and 1984 Yearbook of American Poetry.

She won the first Greensboro Poetry Slam sponsored by the International Poetry Review.

Muriel is past President of Beth David Sisterhood, Greensboro, NC and has written the cover poems for the Beth David Synagogue High Holiday booklet for the past 53 years. She is also a lifetime member of Hadassah and participates in the Women's Cabinet of the Greensboro Jewish Federation.

For more information about Muriel's poetry, please visit her website at www.messagesfrommuriel.com.

www.ingramcontent.com/pod-product-compliance
Lightning Source LLC
Chambersburg PA
CBHW070528010526
44110CB00050B/2251